JAMES COOK
Across the Pacific to Australasia

Clint Twist

Evans Brothers Limited

Evans Brothers Limited
2A Portman Mansions
Chiltern Street
London W1M 1LE

Printed in Hong Kong

ISBN 0 237 51269 5

Series editor: Su Swallow
Editor: Nicola Barber
Designer: Neil Sayer
Production: Jenny Mulvanny

Maps and Illustrations: Brian Watson, Linden Artists

Acknowledgements

For permission to reproduce copyright material the author and
publishers gratefully acknowledge the following:

Cover (top left) Sextant by Jesse Ramsden c.1770, Maritime
Museum, e.t. archive, (top right) Native mask from New Guinea,
e.t.archive, (bottom left) New Zealand Maori jade Hei Tiki,
British Museum, Michael Holford, (bottom right) King Penguins,
South Georgia Island, The Image Bank
Title page National Maritime Museum, Michael Holford
page 4 (top) e.t. archive, (bottom) B. Schledge, ZEFA **page 5**
Paul Harris, Royal Geographical Society **page 6** The British
Library **page 7** H.R. Dörig, Hutchison Library **page 8** Quebec
House, Kent, e.t. archive **page 9** (top) Robert Francis,
Hutchison Library, (bottom) Uffizi Gallery, Florence, e.t. archive
page 10 Royal Society, London, The Bridgeman Art Library
page 11 (left) ZEFA, (right) Royal Geographical Society **page
12** (top) e.t. archive, (bottom) Image Select **page 13** Coal
Meters Committee, London, The Bridgeman Art Library **page
14** Erwin Christian, ZEFA **page 15** City of Bristol Museum and
Art Gallery, The Bridgeman Art Library **page 16** (top) National
Maritime Museum, Michael Holford, (bottom) National Maritime
Museum, The Bridgeman Art Library **page 17** The Bridgeman
Art Library **page 18** (top) The British Library, (bottom) e.t.
archive **page 20** (top) Mary Evans Picture Library, (bottom) The
British Library **page 21** ZEFA **page 22** (top) National Maritime
Museum, Michael Holford, (bottom) British Museum, London,
The Bridgeman Art Library **page 23** Joe van Os, The Image
Bank **page 24** (top) British Museum, London, The Bridgeman
Art Library, (bottom) The Admiralty, e.t. archive **page 25**
National Maritime Museum, e.t. archive **page 26** (top) Bruce
Coleman Limited, (bottom) e.t. archive **page 27** (top) Mary
Evans Picture Library, (bottom) e.t. archive **page 28** (top)
National Library of Australia, e.t. archive, (middle) e.t. archive
page 29 (top) Hulton Deutsch Collection Limited, (bottom)
David Tokeley, Robert Harding Picture Library **page 30** (top)
ZEFA, (middle) Paulo Curto, The Image Bank, (bottom) Mary
Evans Picture Library **page 31** (top) Ian Lloyd, Hutchison
Library, (bottom) Wisniewski, ZEFA **page 32** Anders Ryman
page 33 (top) Don Cole, Compix, (bottom) British Museum,
Michael Holford **page 34** Louvre, Paris, The Bridgeman Art
Library **page 35** (top left) British Museum, Michael Holford,
(top right) Anders Ryman, (bottom) AKG, Image Select **page 36**
(top) D. Baglin, ZEFA, (bottom) John Miles, Royal Geographical
Society **page 37** Rano Raraku, Royal Geographical Society
page 38 (top) Victoria and Albert Museum, e.t. archive,
(bottom) Mary Evans Picture Library **page 39** e.t. archive **page
40** National Maritime Museum, e.t. archive **page 41** (top) ZEFA,
(bottom) National Library of Australia, e.t. archive **page 42**
Bruce Coleman Limited **page 43** (top) Penny Tweedie, Panos
Pictures, (bottom) Robert Harding Picture Library

Contents

Introduction

A portrait of Captain Cook in his Royal Navy uniform painted shortly before his third voyage. Cook's wife did not like the portrait because she thought it made him look too stern.

James Cook first went to sea when he was 18 years old. At that time he was training to be a grocer, but going to sea seemed a far more exciting prospect. Twice Cook worked his way up from ordinary seaman to the rank of captain — once on board merchant ships, and then again in the British navy. Between 1768 and 1779, Cook made three great voyages of exploration. He charted the position of many of the islands in the Pacific Ocean, and almost completed the map of the world. As a result of these voyages, James Cook has become one of the most famous sea captains in history.

Cook's success was due to a combination of experience and skill. By the time he was given command of his own ship he had spent more than 20 years at sea, and there were few tasks aboard ship that he himself had not done. During his early career on merchant ships Cook became an expert navigator and learned how to handle a ship in rough weather. Later, in the navy, he was trained as a surveyor and map-maker and was put to work making accurate charts. He

An Australian koala bear. James Cook was the first European to set foot in Australia, and the first to see many of Australia's unique plants and animals.

Captain Cook sailed to the Hawaiian Islands in 1778. Some parts of the coastline of the Hawaiian Islands are steep cliffs of volcanic rock. In other places there are wide, sandy beaches.

Horizons

After reading this book, you may want to find out more about James Cook's discoveries. Or you might become interested in a particular place or topic. At the end of some of the chapters in this book, you will find **Horizons** boxes. These boxes contain the names of people, places and things which are not mentioned in the book, but which are connected with the story of James Cook. By looking these names up in the indexes of other reference books, you will be able to discover more about Cook and his world.

became so skilled with surveying instruments, and so good at chart-making, that in 1768 he was the natural choice to command the *Endeavour* on a scientific expedition to the island of Tahiti in the Pacific Ocean.

The purpose of this expedition was to observe the movement of the planet Venus through telescopes. But Cook also had other instructions. These were to sail south to see what he could discover, and in particular to see if there was any truth in reports by Dutch sailors about the existence of a place called New Holland (Australia). Before Cook's first voyage, all that was known of Australia was based on an ancient Greek theory, and on a few vague reports of islands and coastlines. Cook's voyage showed that Australia was a huge island continent with its own strange wildlife.

On his second voyage, Cook sailed further south than anyone had before. Steering a course between huge icebergs, he sailed right around the world. Without realising it, Cook sailed around Antarctica, but he was prevented from reaching the coastline of this frozen continent by a solid wall of ice. On his third voyage, Cook discovered the Hawaiian Islands, explored the coastline of Alaska, and sailed on into the Arctic Ocean. Returning to the Hawaiian Islands, he became involved in a bad-tempered argument with the native people of the islands and was killed.

Aside from his discoveries, James Cook also made a long-lasting contribution to the science of navigation. By making use of the latest scientific instruments and information, Cook became the first person to fix the position of remote places accurately. In particular, Cook was the first to establish longitude (position east or west) by taking sightings of the moon and stars.

The historical background

A life at sea

James Cook was born in 1728, in Yorkshire, England. His father worked as a farm manager for a wealthy landowner who paid for James to attend the local school. James did well at his studies, and after leaving school he first went to work in a grocer's and then, in 1746, he went to sea, finding work as a seaman on a merchant ship.

For nearly ten years, Cook worked on ships sailing around the British coast and across the stormy North Sea to Scandinavia. As he gained experience he was promoted, and in 1755 he was offered the command of his own merchant ship. Instead, he joined the British navy as an ordinary seaman. Britain was soon to be at war with France, and Cook may have believed that it was his duty to go and fight.

In fact, Cook saw very little fighting. His abilities as a navigator were soon noted, and he spent most of the war surveying parts of the Canadian coast to make accurate charts for the navy — unexciting work, but very important. After the war, when the British navy was planning a scientific expedition to the Pacific Ocean, James Cook, navigator and surveyor, was chosen to be captain. Part of the reason for this voyage was to try to discover new and distant lands. In this, Cook was part of a long European tradition of overseas exploration.

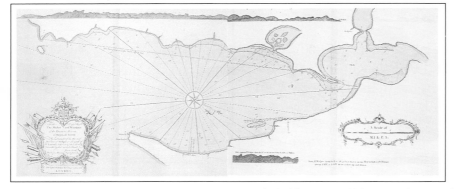

The first chart (sea map) by Captain Cook to be published, in 1758. The chart shows the Bay of Gaspé in Canada.

Overseas explorations

During the 15th and 16th centuries, sea captains sailing from Spain and Portugal made a series of great exploring voyages. Columbus reached America, da Gama found a sea route to India, and Magellan's ships sailed right around the world. These voyages opened the way for conquest and trade as European soldiers and merchants also set out across the oceans. Both Spain and Portugal began to establish large overseas empires.

Spain was already the most powerful country in Europe, and it soon became the wealthiest as huge quantities of gold and silver were shipped back from Central and South America. In addition, America had large areas of good farmland suitable for cattle ranching and plantation crops such as sugar cane and cotton. Thousands of Spanish settlers sailed across the Atlantic Ocean to start a new life in New Spain (present-day Mexico).

The Portuguese Empire developed in a different way. There were discoveries of gold and silver in Africa and India, but the supplies quickly dried up. Instead, Portugal found another form of wealth. Most of the exotic spices and flavourings used in European cookery, for example pepper, cloves, and cinnamon, were grown in India and the Spice Islands (the present-day Molucca Islands in Indonesia). By controlling the trade in these spices, Portugal became nearly as rich as Spain.

Spain and Portugal were not the only European countries interested in exotic lands overseas. As news of the first discoveries spread, French, English and Dutch captains also set out on voyages of exploration, settlement and trade. By 1700, Spain, Portugal, France, England and the Netherlands had established worldwide trading empires. These overseas empires made all five nations both rich and powerful.

Peruvian gold brought back by the Spanish from their empire in South America

The balance of power

In 1700, the balance of power between European nations was upset by the death of Charles II, the Spanish king. Before he died, Charles named a French prince to be his successor (the next king). The French were delighted by this, because it would make France the most powerful country in Europe. The other European nations were not so pleased, and argued with France. These arguments led to what is called the War of the Spanish

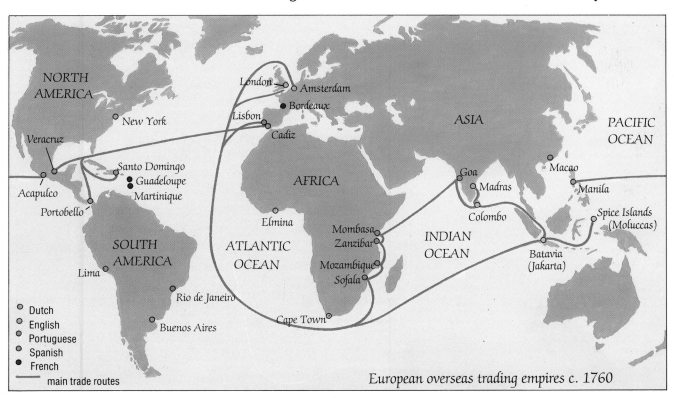

European overseas trading empires c. 1760

Dutch
English
Portuguese
Spanish
French
— main trade routes

A contemporary picture showing British soldiers capturing the Canadian town of Quebec from the French

Succession (1701-13). This war was fought between France and Spain on one side, and the rest of Europe (Portugal, England, the Netherlands, Austria and most of Germany) on the other. Although most of the fighting took place in Belgium and northern France, there were battles as far away as Spain and Italy. By the end of the war, even some of the distant overseas territories had become involved.

France and Spain lost the war, and they signed a peace treaty with the other European nations. Under this treaty, both France and Spain lost territory. All the countries on the winning side were rewarded, but it was England that came off best. During the war, England had united with Scotland to form the United Kingdom of Great Britain. The peace treaty of 1713 greatly increased the power of the newly united Great Britain.

The first half of the 18th century saw a series of European wars. Out of these wars two countries, France and Britain, emerged as rivals for world power. Both countries had large navies and possessed overseas territories in North America, the West Indies and India. In 1754, rivalry between British and French settlers in North America turned into armed conflict. Under the command of James Wolfe, British soldiers captured the city of Quebec in 1759 where Wolfe was killed. The British went on to capture Montreal (in 1760), and to force the French to leave Canada. In the West Indies, several important French islands, including Martinique and Guadeloupe, were attacked and seized by British warships.

In Europe a war was fought on land and at sea between the British and the French. France and its allies were eventually defeated after a long series of battles. In India, under the command of Robert Clive, British troops defeated a French-Indian army and established British rule over nearly the whole of the Indian subcontinent. By 1763, the French had been defeated

A statue of Ferdinand Magellan. It stands in the Chilean port of Punta Arenas, on the Strait of Magellan

The famous Italian scientist, Galileo Galilei

on four continents (they had also lost their trading posts in Africa), and asked for a peace treaty.

The conditions of the Treaty of Paris (1763) made Britain the most powerful country in the world. This small island off the coast of northern Europe now ruled an empire that stretched from North America to India. When James Cook sailed in 1768 he was to 'discover' a continent previously unknown to Europeans that would increase Britain's wealth and power still further.

The scientific approach

As well as bringing power and wealth to Europe, overseas discoveries also had another important effect — they encouraged people to believe in the importance of a scientific approach to questions about the world around them. In 1492, Columbus sailed west because he believed that the world was round like a ball. This was a revolutionary idea at the time, because most people thought that the earth was flat. Then, in 1522, the completion of the first circumnavigation of the globe by Magellan's ships proved that the world was round. This voyage was a great feat of navigation and exploration, but it was also a great victory for science.

The gradual shift towards a scientific approach among educated people in Europe happened during the 16th and 17th centuries. Before this time, most scholars accepted the teachings of the Christian Church that questions about the world around them could be explained by the answer: 'Because God made the world like that.' Slowly, scholars began to understand that nature follows certain laws and rules. By studying these laws and rules, scholars began to gain a greater understanding of how nature works. This method of studying and thinking is called the scientific approach.

Between 1550 and 1750 European scholars made a series of great discoveries by using the scientific approach. In Italy, the astronomer and mathematician Galileo Galilei (1564-1642) used experiments and observation to establish the mathematical laws that govern the motion of falling objects and swinging objects (pendulums). Galileo also supported the theory put forward by Nicolas Copernicus (1473-1543) that the earth moves around the sun (at that time, people believed that the sun and the planets all circled around the earth). But the Catholic Church objected to Galileo's work, and even put him in prison for a time to prevent him from continuing with it.

In Protestant Germany, however, Johannes Kepler (1571-1630) was able to show by mathematics that the planets did move around the sun. He also established scientific laws that explained how the planets moved in space. In England, Isaac Newton

(1642-1727) took this work even further and established the scientific laws that govern all moving objects. He also proposed a theory of gravitation (gravity), which explains why objects fall to the ground.

Scientific measurement

The increase in scientific knowledge was helped by the invention of instruments that allowed scientists to observe nature more closely, and measure it more accurately. For example, the simple telescope was invented some time during the period 1550 to 1600. It consisted of two or more lenses in a straight tube. Many people, including Galileo, have been credited with the invention of the telescope, but we cannot be certain who actually made the first 'distance viewer'.

An efficient microscope ('small viewer') was invented in 1673 by the Dutch scientist Anton van Leeuwenhoek (1632-1723). Many scientists used this new invention to study the details of natural things and processes. In 1644, an Italian named Evangelista Torricelli (1608-47) invented the mercury barometer. This instrument measures atmospheric pressure (the weight of the air above). In 1714, the German scientist Gabriel Fahrenheit invented the mercury thermometer, which could measure temperature accurately. Other new inventions were also made, for example the accurate time-keeper (see page 16). When James Cook set sail in 1768, all of these instruments were available to the captain of a scientific voyage.

Newton invented the reflecting telescope in which light is reflected by a curved mirror at the bottom of the tube to an eye-piece mounted on the side.

Terra Australis

Australia was invented by the ancient Greeks because it appealed to their sense of symmetry. The Greeks had a fairly good idea of the geography of land stretching hundreds of kilometres to the north, south and east of the Mediterranean Sea. They also knew roughly the shape and position of Africa and India. Beyond that, they knew nothing — rather like Europeans at the time of Columbus.

However, the Greeks observed that natural things were often symmetrical (made up of two identical halves). The Greeks knew that the northern half of the world contained a large land mass (Europe and Asia), so they reasoned that the southern half of the world should also contain a great continent. The Greeks gave this continent a name — *Terra Australis*, which means 'Southern Land' — even though they did not know for certain that it really existed. In Europe, this idea persisted until Cook discovered Australia.

The first map to show part of Australia was drawn at the beginning of the 17th century by a Dutch navigator. 'Australia' is the short stretch of yellow coastline in the bottom right-hand corner.

The island of Tahiti

Horizons

You could find out about some of the scientists and inventors who lived around the same time as James Cook: Edmund Cartwright (invented the power loom); Henry Cavendish (physicist and chemist); Luigi Galvani (experimented with electricity); William Hargreaves (invented a spinning machine); Jacques and Joseph Montgolfier (built and flew the first hot-air balloon).

Pacific voyages

Ferdinand Magellan first sailed into the Pacific Ocean in 1520, and other sea captains soon followed him. However, the records of where these sailors went and what they found are not always clear. One of the reasons for this was the rivalry between European nations. Sea captains usually had strict instructions to keep their discoveries secret. When the discovery of a new place was reported, its position was often not given very accurately. This was because navigators did not yet have a reliable system for measuring longitude. The French, for example, discovered the islands of Samoa, only to lose them again for nearly 200 years because they recorded their position inaccurately.

Until Cook sailed, Europeans had only vague ideas about what was in the Pacific. The Dutch navigator Abel Tasman (1603-59) had sighted New Zealand, and part of what he called New Holland (Australia), but he was unable to get closer. The English sailor William Dampier (1652-1715) had also reported sighting the coastline of what might have been New Holland. In 1767, a British ship discovered the islands of Tahiti. By a fortunate coincidence, Tahiti was the perfect place from which to observe the planet Venus as it moved across the face of the sun in the following year. Tahiti also happened to be a good place from which to set out on an exploration to find New Holland.

Transport and technology

Ships of the line in action in 1782 during the Battle of the Saintes between the British and French fleets in the West Indies

The pressgang used to wait outside harbour taverns and seize 'recruits' for the navy.

The Royal Navy

When James Cook went to sea, he was following a seafaring tradition that went back hundreds of years. No part of Britain is more than about 120 kilometres from the sea, and ships were a cheap and reliable method of transporting goods from one part of the country to another. In Cook's day, for example, coal was taken by sea from northern England along the coast and up the River Thames to London. The sea also allowed Britain to trade with other countries. Before the 16th century, this trade was confined to Europe, the Mediterranean and Scandinavia. However, from the 16th century onwards, British ships were to be found in ports all over the world.

As sea power became more important in Europe, so did the British navy. By Cook's day, the British navy was known as the Royal Navy. Apart from defending the British Isles, the Royal Navy was expected to organise supplies for naval bases around the world, send warships to patrol trade routes and escort merchant ships, and protect British citizens and outposts.

In 1768, the Royal Navy had hundreds of ships. The most important, the battleships of their day, were the ships of the line. They were called ships of the line because naval battles were often fought between warships arranged in straight lines. A typical ship of the line was about 55 metres long and had three masts, with a sloping bowsprit at the bow (front). There were three decks which carried at least 64 cannons. The largest ships of the line had more than 100 cannons, about 40 of which could be fired together in a broadside at the same target. To sail the ship and fire the guns, a ship of the line had a crew of at least 500 sailors. Some of these sailors were boys as young as ten years old. Most ships of the line also carried a detachment of marines (naval soldiers) who took no part in the running of the ship.

For the ordinary sailors and marines, life below decks was crowded, dirty and unpleasant. Not surprisingly, there was usually a shortage of sailors. Like other European nations at this time, the British often put people in the navy against their will. Men in British harbour towns were often kidnapped by groups of sailors (called 'the pressgang') and forced to work aboard Royal Navy ships.

A collier unloading coal into a smaller boat on the River Thames, London

Captain Cook's ship, the *Endeavour*

The *Endeavour*

To sail to distant Tahiti, the navy chose a type of ship known as a Whitby collier, or cat collier. Whitby colliers were not designed to sail distant oceans, but to carry coal through the storms and waves of the North Sea. They were, however, strongly built ships. A collier was a good choice of ship for Cook because he had sailed aboard several colliers as a young seaman, and he knew them well.

Cook's ship, the *Endeavour*, had three masts and three decks, but at 30 metres in length it was smaller than a ship of the line. The cargo hold was converted to carry the stores of food and water that the expedition would need on its long voyage. Although the voyage was not for military purposes, the *Endeavour* was a navy ship and was fitted with cannons. Altogether, the ship carried 94 people — 85 in the crew and nine in the scientific party. Besides the officers and ordinary seamen, the crew included carpenters, sail-makers, rope-makers, cooks and cabin boys. There were also 12 marines who had their own officer and drummer boy. The scientific party included a botanist, two naturalists, an astronomer and several artists who were to provide a visual record of the voyage.

Outrigger canoes are still used around many Pacific islands today.

Pacific canoes

When Cook arrived in Tahiti he saw that the people of the Pacific islands were no strangers to the sea. Trade between islands separated by hundred of kilometres of ocean was quite common. To travel between islands, the native peoples of the Pacific used the outrigger canoe, powered either by paddles or by a single sail.

An outrigger canoe had a long float attached to one side by wooden poles. This float (the outrigger) made the canoe more stable as it sailed across the ocean waves. Most Pacific island canoes were quite small, each capable of carrying about a dozen people. However, large double canoes were also built. These canoes had two hulls of up to 30 metres in length, fastened together side-by-side. Double canoes could carry the large amounts of food needed for the longest voyages. They were also used as war canoes, and a large double canoe could take up to 100 armed warriors.

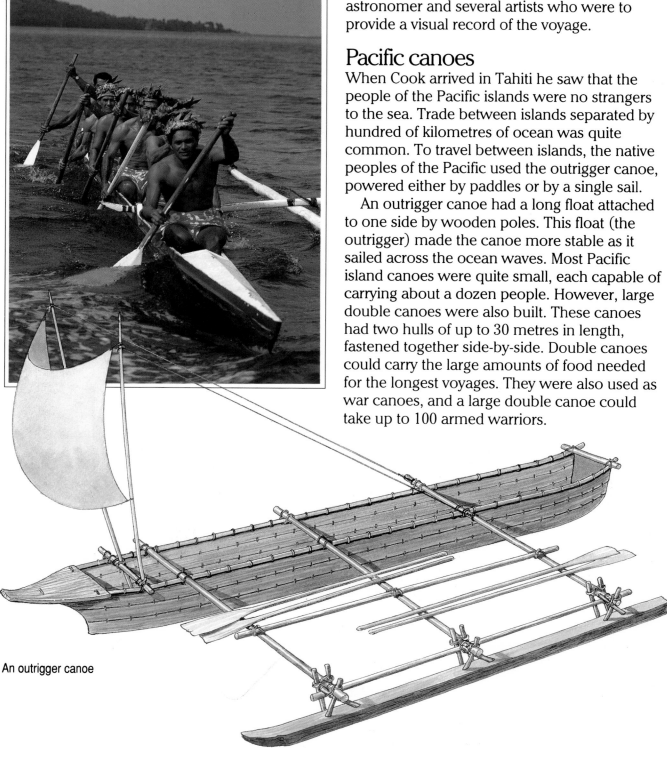

An outrigger canoe

A portrait of Joseph Banks, painted towards the end of his life

Joseph Banks

One of the scientists on board the *Endeavour*, the botanist Joseph Banks (1743-1820), became for a time even more famous than James Cook. Banks was a young man of 25 when he sailed with Cook, and he was full of enthusiasm for botany (the scientific study of plants). He was also very rich, and paid the expenses of most of the scientific party. Joseph Banks was fortunate to sail with Cook aboard the *Endeavour*. The voyage was to take them to places never before visited by Europeans, and Banks was able to examine many new plant species. He was also the first scientist to observe and describe the strange animal wildlife of Australia (see page 29).

When the *Endeavour* returned to Britain, Banks's reports and descriptions of what he had seen soon made him famous. He started to write a book about the plants and animals of Australia, but he became enthusiastic about another expedition, this time to Iceland, and his book about Australia was never finished.

The transit of Venus. Seen from Earth, the planet Venus appears to move across the face of the Sun.

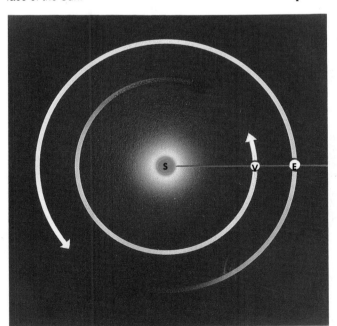

Astronomy and navigation

The Royal Navy was paying for the voyage of the *Endeavour*, and it had little or no interest in strange plants and animals. However, the navy was interested in navigation and in the movement of the stars and planets. Scientists knew from their calculations that, during June 1769, the planet Venus would appear to transit (move across) the face of the sun. If they could observe and measure this event, then they could use this measurement to calculate the distance between the earth and the sun. The only difficulty was that the best place to observe the transit of Venus was the island of Tahiti in the Pacific Ocean. The Royal Navy agreed to send a ship.

In order to take accurate measurements, it was necessary to know the exact position of Tahiti. This was the task given to James Cook — find a small island in the middle of a vast ocean, and then work out where it is on the map.

From the earliest times, people have used the sun and stars to navigate their way across the sea. Over the centuries, a number of devices were devised to help navigators find their way more accurately, for example the backstaff and cross-staff. By Cook's time, position north or south was calculated with the aid of a sextant.

Cook was the first navigator to establish longitude (position east or west) accurately. He was able to do this largely because of the invention of an accurate time-keeper. By the middle of the 18th century, scientists knew quite a lot about the world. They knew that the earth was round, and they had calculated its dimensions. They could chart the course of the moon as it moved across the night sky, and they knew that this course varied slightly on each day of the year. By using this information, they could calculate the position of the sun (or any other star) as seen from any place in the world at any particular time. This information was published in great lists of times and positions called celestial almanacs. Special lists for use at sea were called nautical almanacs. By using almanacs and sextants, navigators could tell where they were if they knew exactly what the time was. The problem was that accurate pendulum clocks (called chronometers) would not work on board ship because of the movement of the waves.

In 1714, the Royal Navy announced a competition with a large cash prize for the first person to make a chronometer suitable for a ship. The prize was eventually won by a carpenter named John Harrison, who gave up woodwork and began to make metal clocks instead. Cook took a chronometer designed by Harrison with him on his voyages. This chronometer was so accurate that the error was less than five seconds per month, and this could be taken into consideration when doing calculations. By combining the accuracy of the chronometer, the lists in the nautical almanacs and his skills with a sextant, Cook was able to establish the position of his ship much more precisely than anyone had before.

Cook measured longitude in degrees east or west of a map line running north-south through the English town of Greenwich (now part of London). North-south map lines are called meridians. At first, other countries measured longitude according to

The dividers and rulers used by Captain Cook to draw lines and measure distances on charts

Harrison's chronometer. This was the first portable clock to keep time with sufficient accuracy to be used for navigation.

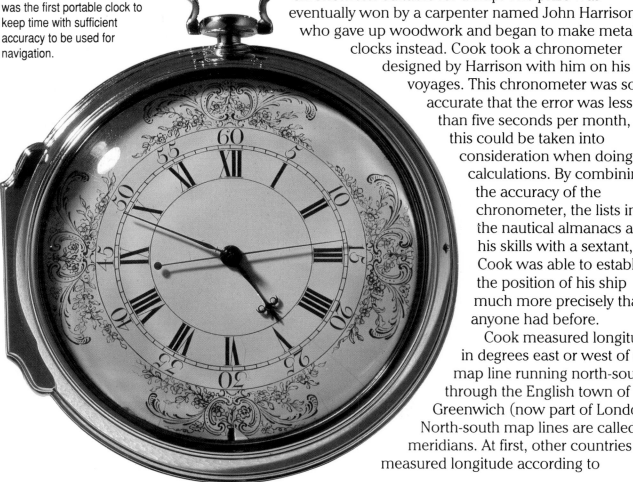

Clocks

Mechanical clocks did not appear in Europe until the end of the 13th century. The first clocks were large (about two metres high) and were not very accurate. Most people preferred to use traditional sundials for telling the time during the day. Small sundials could even be carried around in the pocket. In 1657, the Dutch scientist Christiaan Huygens invented the pendulum clock which used a swinging pendulum to keep accurate time. Pendulum clocks were ideal for houses and public buildings, but they would only keep going if they were kept perfectly still. They were of little use to travellers, and even less use on board a ship which was constantly rocking on the waves.

Portable clocks, driven by springs, were introduced during the 17th century. At first, these spring-driven 'clockwork' clocks were very inaccurate. Even the best ones needed to be adjusted at least once a week. Not until the chronometer was developed during the 1760s did accurate, portable time-keeping become possible.

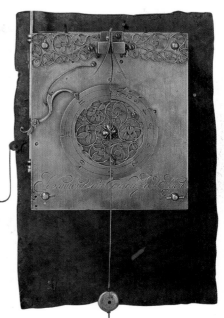

An early pendulum clock by Huygens

meridians running through their own territory. In 1884, an international treaty established the Greenwich Meridian as the one to be used on all future maps. Longitude is now measured in degrees (1°-180°) east or west of Greenwich.

The benefit of experience

When he was asked to plan more voyages across the Pacific, Cook was able to make several useful suggestions based on the experience of his first voyage. Cook now believed that one ship was not enough for such a voyage. When sailing in shallow water, a single ship was too vulnerable to the dangers of a hidden reef which could tear a hole in the hull. If this happened, a second ship would be able to rescue the crew of the damaged ship. For his other voyages, Cook chose two more Whitby colliers which were re-named the *Resolution* and the *Adventure*.

Another matter on Cook's mind was the prevention of scurvy. This was a disease caused by a lack of vitamin C (found in fresh fruit and vegetables). Cook's own method of trying to prevent scurvy was to issue his crew with sauerkraut (pickled cabbage) and a syrup made of oranges and lemons. Neither the sauerkraut nor the syrup were very effective because pickling and cooking both destroy most of the vitamin C. British navy doctors had another method they wanted to try out. During his second voyage, Cook agreed to give all of his crew a spoonful of specially prepared carrot marmalade each day. This delicious concoction was another failure. A few years later, the British navy settled on lime juice as a successful method of taking vitamin C to sea. This earned British sailors the nickname 'limeys'.

The voyages of James Cook

First command

The *Endeavour* sailed from England on 25 August 1768 under the command of Lieutenant James Cook. Four weeks later, Cook called at Madeira to take on fresh supplies. He then crossed the Atlantic Ocean to Rio de Janeiro in Brazil. Turning south, the *Endeavour* sailed around Cape Horn through the stormy seas of the South Atlantic, reaching the Pacific Ocean in February 1769.

A sketch of the *Endeavour* in rough seas made by one of the crew

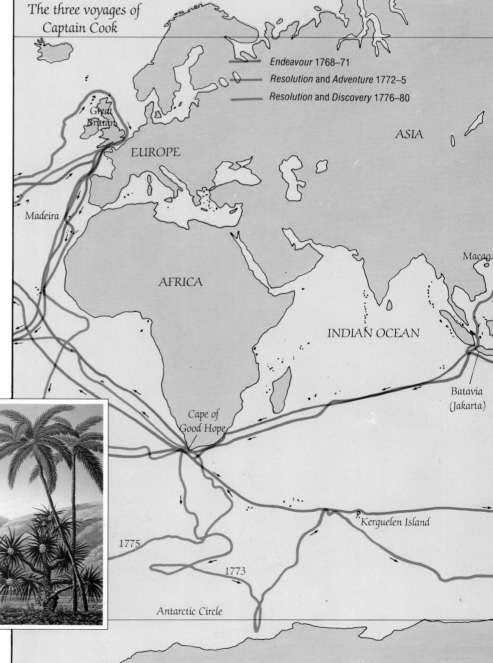

The three voyages of Captain Cook

— Endeavour 1768–71
— Resolution and Adventure 1772–5
— Resolution and Discovery 1776–80

EUROPE
ASIA
AFRICA
INDIAN OCEAN
Great Britain
Madeira
Macao
Batavia (Jakarta)
Cape of Good Hope
Kerguelen Island
1775
1773
Antarctic Circle

A painting of a Tahitian village with people wearing typical native dress

The expedition sailed across the Pacific for two months before making landfall at Tahiti on 13 April. Cook established friendly relations with the native inhabitants of the island, offering beads, metal tools and nails in exchange for fresh food. Sometimes the Tahitians stole small items — Cook even had a pair of socks stolen from beneath his pillow while he slept. When a Tahitian snatched a musket from one of the British marines, the other sailors shot and killed the thief. Cook was very anxious to avoid any more incidents like this, and he quickly made peace with the native people. However, to protect the scientists and their equipment, Cook ordered his men to build a small log fort. When it was finished, it could accommodate 45 people.

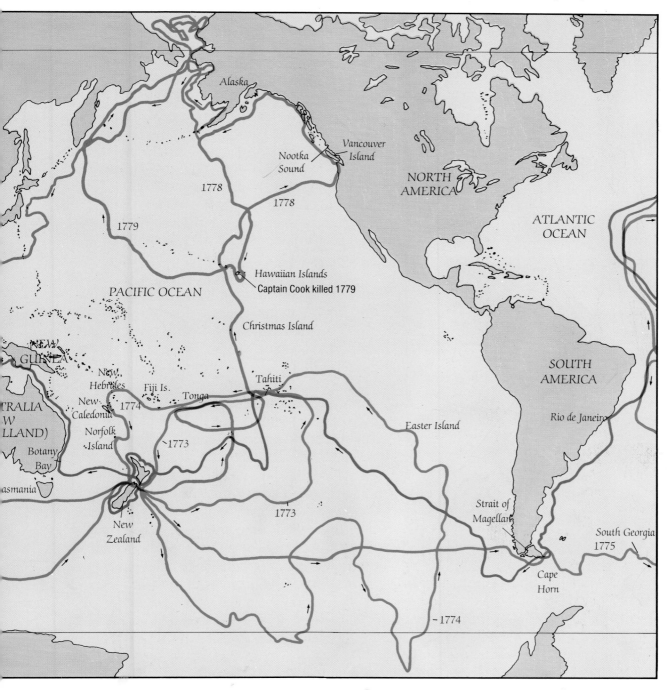

A New Zealand war canoe of the type that threatened the crew of the *Endeavour*

Secret instructions

On 3 June 1769, the scientists had perfect weather to observe the transit of Venus. From nine o'clock in the morning until about half past three, Cook and the scientists watched the planet as it moved across the face of the sun. Banks and the other naturalists then spent another six weeks collecting specimens, while Cook planned the rest of the voyage. He had secret orders from the British government to explore the Pacific in search of New Holland.

Cook decided to sail first to New Zealand. The existence of New Zealand had been reported by Tasman in 1642, but very little was known about it. Cook set sail in the middle of July, taking along a Tahitian man who had volunteered himself as a guide and interpreter, even though he had never visited New Zealand. The *Endeavour* sighted land during the first week in October, and a small party went ashore by boat. This time the native people were not friendly and attacked the sailors. Later, through the Tahitian interpreter, Cook did manage to talk to some of the New Zealand people, whose language was very like that of the Tahitians. Some trade took place, but neither side really trusted the other. Setting sail once more, Cook was determined to make an accurate chart of New Zealand. For five months he sailed a figure-of-eight course around New Zealand, proving that it was made up of two large islands. The chart that Cook produced was so complete and so accurate that it remained in use for nearly 100 years.

Cook then turned westwards towards the reported position of New Holland. Although several Dutch and British ships had visited parts of the coast, nobody knew whether it was one very large island or several small islands. Land was sighted on 20 April 1770. The sailors saw figures standing on the shore and smoke from cooking fires. But it was not until a week later that Cook found a suitable place to anchor, and a party could go ashore. The native people showed little interest in the visitors, and most of them ran off as the landing party approached the shore. They appeared to be much more primitive than the Tahitians or New Zealanders, and spoke a completely different language.

Banks was delighted with what he found in this new country. There were so many strange plant species that he could scarcely count them. Cook was so impressed that he named the place Botany Bay. There were also some new animals, including the kangaroo.

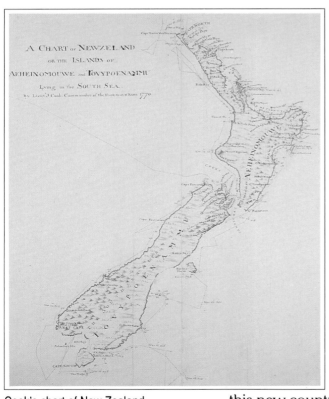

Cook's chart of New Zealand

The *Endeavour* then sailed northwards along the coast. By mid-June the ship was in a narrow corridor of water between a huge reef and the shore. Late one night, the ship sailed into the reef and stuck fast. After 23 hours the crew managed to pull the ship off the reef, but there was a large hole in the hull. The crew patched the hole by hauling a spare sail over the side. Fortunately the sail plugged the hole, and the ship remained afloat long enough to reach land, which was about 30 kilometres away.

It took nearly two months to carry out makeshift repairs. The *Endeavour* then continued northwards, slowly finding a way through the reef. By the end of August, Cook had mapped most of Australia's western coastline. Cook then sailed south of New Guinea and on to the Dutch port of Batavia (Jakarta) in Indonesia so that the *Endeavour* could be repaired properly. While the repairs were being made fever broke out among the crew, and more than 20 of them died. Cook had to hire extra sailors for the journey home.

On 12th July 1771, the *Endeavour* finally returned to Britain. Cook received a hero's welcome and was promoted by the Royal Navy, becoming Captain James Cook.

The Great Barrier Reef off Australia's eastern coast. The *Endeavour* was stuck for 23 hours on underwater rocks in the reef.

The second voyage

For his next voyage Cook had two new ships, the *Resolution* and the *Adventure*. The main purpose of this voyage was to sail across the southern Pacific Ocean in order to find out if there was another continent even further south than Australia and New Zealand. Cook referred to this unknown land as the great 'Southern Continent'. Cook also intended to investigate the position of several islands that had been reported by Dutch, Spanish and French navigators.

Cook left England again on 13 July 1772. He sailed south, stopping at Madeira and Cape Horn to pick up fresh supplies. As the two ships continued south past the tip of Africa, they soon sighted huge icebergs. It quickly became very cold, and the crew were given thick woollen jackets and trousers to wear. As they sailed further south, the icebergs increased in numbers. Although the icebergs were a menace to the ships, they did have one advantage: the sailors could melt pieces of ice to make fresh drinking water.

On 17 January 1773, the two ships crossed what we now call the Antarctic Circle (about 66° south). Nobody had ever sailed so far south before. Shortly afterwards, the ships became separated in thick fog. Cook and the captain of the *Adventure* had agreed to make for New Zealand if this should happen and, at the beginning of April, Cook found the *Adventure* waiting for him there.

Return to Tahiti

Cook then steered a looping course through unexplored waters to Tahiti. But the ships stayed in Tahiti for only about a month before Cook took them back to New Zealand by a different route. On the way, they visited the islands of Tonga where they were warmly welcomed with feasts, and songs from the young Tongan women. Cook considered the people of Tonga to be the friendliest in the Pacific, and greatly admired their well-organised system of agriculture.

After leaving Tonga the ships became separated again, this time in a storm. Cook was forced to stop in New Zealand to repair some storm damage, and after leaving a message sealed in a bottle for the *Adventure*, he decided that the *Resolution* should carry on alone. He sailed south until he was among the icebergs, continuing his search for the Southern Continent. The weather was very cold, and

Captain Cook's ships, the *Resolution* and the *Adventure*, at anchor in Tahiti

This feather headdress was presented to Captain Cook by the people of Tahiti.

most of the ship became covered with a layer of ice. The crew had nothing to eat except salt beef and two-year-old biscuits. Slowly Cook continued south, but by the end of January 1774 the way was blocked by a solid wall of ice. Cook reluctantly turned back, having reached a latitude of 71° south.

Island hopping

Cook decided to return to Tahiti to pick up fresh supplies before continuing across the Pacific. On the way, he was able to confirm the existence of Easter Island, which had been reported and named by a Dutch explorer, Jacob Roggeveen, in 1722. Cook recognised it as the same island because of the huge statues, some up to ten metres tall, that stood all over the island.

Penguins on the island of South Georgia. The island was discovered by Captain Cook in 1775.

When Cook arrived at Tahiti, he found the Tahitians preparing for war against a neighbouring island. The Europeans were astonished by the Tahitian war fleet of more than 100 canoes, each over 20 metres long. However, the Europeans did not stay to watch the hostilities but left at the end of June. At this point, Cook began to make some discoveries of his own. His first discovery was some small islands which he named New Caledonia. About a thousand kilometres further on he found Norfolk Island, which was later to become a vital source of timber for settlers in Australia.

After calling at New Zealand, Cook decided to sail eastwards in order to explore the southern part of the Atlantic Ocean. There he discovered the ice-covered islands of Georgia and South Georgia. Finally, Cook sailed back to Britain, arriving on 29 July 1775. He found that the *Adventure* had also returned safely, reaching British waters about one year before the *Resolution*.

The third voyage

Only a year later, Cook set off on another voyage of exploration. For his third voyage, Cook planned to sail across the Pacific Ocean and search for a sea route around the top of North America. The possibility of such a route had fascinated navigators for over 200 years, and Cook believed that he could find the 'northwest passage', as it was known.

Once again, Cook sailed aboard the *Resolution*, and took with him another Whitby collier named the *Discovery*. The two ships left separately, and arranged to meet up at the southern tip of Africa to take on fresh supplies. In fact, the *Resolution* sailed from Britain on 12th July 1776. This was just eight days after the American Declaration of Independence — an event that was to have an enormous effect on Britain — but Cook sailed before the news had crossed the Atlantic.

From South Africa the two ships sailed to New Zealand, and on the way Cook was able to confirm the position of Kerguelen Island in the Indian Ocean which had been discovered by a French explorer, Yves Kerguelen de Trémarec. Leaving New Zealand in February 1777, Cook decided that it was already too late to sail to the far north that year, so he went first to Tonga, then to Tahiti, spending several months at each group of islands.

The *Resolution* and the *Discovery* eventually set out from Tahiti across the Pacific Ocean at the beginning of December. On 24 December the crews sighted a small island, which was immediately named Christmas Island. They stayed for only a day or so, long enough to catch fish and over 300 sea turtles for food. The two ships then continued their voyage northwards.

About a month later, more than 4000 kilometres from Tahiti, Cook discovered a group of islands that are today called the

A carved wooden cup made by the people of Hawaii

Hawaiian Islands. The native Hawaiians appeared to be similar to the inhabitants of other Pacific islands visited by Cook. The Europeans quickly established good relations with the Hawaiians, trading iron nails and tools for supplies of sweet potatoes and yams. After leaving Hawaii, Cook sailed for five weeks across empty ocean before sighting the North American coast (the shores of what is now the state of Oregon, USA). Sailing northwards, the ships anchored off Vancouver Island. Here, the crews traded with the native inhabitants, called the Nootka, swapping metal items for food and furs.

The frozen north

The Nootka were unable to help Cook in his search for the northwest passage, so he was forced to rely on maps published by Russian navigators. Russian hunters had been visiting this area for years, trapping wild animals for their furs. One of the Russian maps showed that Alaska was an island, and Cook hoped that this was correct because the sea passage would give him an easy route to the north.

Unfortunately, the Russian map was wrong and Cook had to sail right around the coast of Alaska, often in foggy weather which made navigation extremely difficult. In August 1778, the two ships sailed from the Pacific Ocean into the Arctic Ocean, and steered a course to the north. After a week, they were faced with the solid frozen wall of an ice field. Several of the crew, including Cook, recognised the ice field from their experiences far to the south on the previous voyage. With winter approaching they knew that they could continue no further, and Cook decided to return to Hawaii to wait for the following spring.

Whilst in the Arctic, some of the crew went off in small boats to hunt walruses for food.

An untimely death

Between November 1778 and the beginning of February 1779 the ships remained at anchor in the Hawaiian Islands, and the crews traded peacefully with the Hawaiians. A week after they sailed north again a sudden storm damaged the *Resolution*, and, unwillingly, Cook was forced to return to Hawaii to make repairs.

Cook was worried that he had outstayed his welcome in Hawaii, and some of the Hawaiians did not seem pleased to see the ships back again so soon. On 14 February Cook went ashore to try to reclaim one of the ship's boats that had been stolen by the Hawaiians. By this time, Cook had become decidedly bad-tempered. Normally he was careful not to offend the native peoples of the places he visited, and he disliked using force against them. However, the various frustrations of the voyage — the incorrect Russian map, the ice field, the storm that damaged the *Resolution* — made him careless this time.

Cook was walking through a crowd of well-armed Hawaiians when one of them made a threatening gesture with a dagger. Cook shot at him, but instead of running away, the crowd attacked. Cook fired again and turned to run. As he ran he was hit on the head with a club and stabbed in the neck with a spear. He fell to the ground and was soon dead. Four marines were also killed in the attack, but the rest of the party managed to return to the ships.

One of the many paintings of the death of Captain Cook at the hands of the Hawaiian islanders

The next day, the two sides talked under a flag of truce. The Hawaiians agreed to return Cook's body and the British agreed to leave peacefully. Eventually, some of Cook's bones were returned and these were buried at sea on 21 February.

The *Resolution* and the *Discovery* made another attempt to explore the Arctic Ocean. However, once again the ships were forced to turn back by thick ice. They sailed south along the coast of Asia to Macao, a Portuguese territory on the coast of China. Here the crews learned that the American Declaration of Independence had led to war. Britain was now fighting against America, France and Spain. They became worried that the *Resolution* and the *Discovery* would be attacked by enemy warships as they sailed back to Britain. In fact, the commanders of the American, French and Spanish navies had all given instructions that Cook's ships were not to be attacked because of the scientific importance of his work. It is a pity that Cook did not live long enough to learn of this international tribute to his navigational skills.

In October 1780, after a voyage of four years and three months, the *Resolution* and the *Discovery* finally returned to England. News of Cook's death had arrived before them, and he was mourned as a national hero.

Horizons

You could find out about some of the other navigators who have explored the Pacific Ocean: Alvaro de Mendaña (Spanish); Pedro de Quiros (Portuguese); Luis Vaez de Torres (Spanish); Louis-Antoine Bougainville (French); Jacob Roggeveen (Dutch); Thor Heyerdahl (Norwegian).

Cook's discoveries

The coastline of Antarctica is surrounded by thick ice fields and pack ice.

The world map completed

James Cook was the greatest sailor of his time. He sailed as far south and as far north as it was possible to go by ship. During his three great voyages, Cook crisscrossed the Pacific Ocean, sailing thousands of kilometres across waters previously unexplored by Europeans. Thanks to James Cook, the map of the Pacific — and of the whole world — was now almost complete. Although he had failed to find the great Southern Continent he had mapped Australia and New Zealand, and fixed the position of many of the Pacific islands.

We now know that there is a Southern Continent — Antarctica. Nearly all of Antarctica is permanently covered by a thick layer of ice and snow, and the continent is surrounded by thick ice fields and pack ice. The exploration of Antarctica did not begin until about 100 years after Cook's death.

The prize of exploration

James Cook sailed on voyages of scientific exploration, not political conquest. Whenever he came across settled and organised peoples he recognised the authority of their leaders. Cook liked the native people he met, and most of the time he treated them with great respect. In particular, Cook and his companions were concerned that the peoples of the Pacific would be corrupted by contact with Europeans. Even as he established trade with them, Cook worried that he was destroying their traditional way of life. However, Cook could be confident that the British government would not want to conquer any of the Pacific islands because there was no

Mai

By far the most famous of Cook's 'discoveries' in his own time was Mai, a young Tahitian man. Mai left his island to accompany Cook's expedition as an interpreter (see page 20) and eventually sailed back to Britain on one of Cook's ships.

Mai caused a tremendous stir in Britain. He was tall and good-looking, and he quickly learned British manners. He became a popular guest at parties, and he was even introduced to the British king. Later, when Cook took Mai back to Tahiti, the two quarrelled because Cook refused to help Mai in a local war.

A portrait of Mai

A prison hulk: an old ship converted into a prison

Part of the 'First Fleet' anchored after its arrival in Australia. One of the first houses built by the convicts is visible on the shore.

advantage in doing so. The islands were too small and too overcrowded to be suitable for settlement. Cook came to the conclusion that the best use for the Pacific islands was as supply stops for British ships.

Australia, however, was a different matter entirely. With over 7.5 million square kilometres of land, Australia was a real prize, and thanks to James Cook the British had a better claim to it than any other nation. At first nobody in Britain was particularly interested in Australia because Britain already had a huge empire in North America and India. But events in America were soon to have a remarkable effect on the future of Australia.

The 'First Fleet'

During the 18th century, the British legal system had very harsh penalties. A person could be hanged for stealing even small items such as a shirt or a pair of shoes. However, many convicted criminals, or 'convicts', were not executed, they were transported instead. Before 1776, large numbers of British convicts were transported by ship to America where they were made to work on farms and plantations. After the American Declaration of Independence in 1776, the Americans refused to accept any more convicts, and the British government needed to find somewhere else to send them. At first convicts were kept on hulks (old ships) anchored in river estuaries and harbours. But the hulks soon became overcrowded, and the government looked for a new place to which they could transport the convicts. In 1785, the government decided that Cook's great discovery — Australia — would be a suitable place for transported convicts. Two years later, the first British fleet carrying convicts set sail for Australia.

The 'First Fleet' (as it is known to Australians) arrived in Botany Bay on 20 January 1788. There were 11 ships carrying some 759 convicts (men, women and a few children) together with about 200 guards, soldiers and officers. The first choice for the

Loads of Australian wool were transported overland to Sydney for export.

Sydney, pictured in 1823 when it was still a small settlement

site of the colony, chosen on Cook's advice, was not a success. The convicts and their guards soon moved a few kilometres along the coast where conditions were much better. Some time later this place was named Sydney (after a British politician), and it is now Australia's largest city.

The new colony grew steadily in size as more convicts arrived, and those already there started families. Between 1801 and 1803, a surveyor named Mathew Flinders sailed around Australia and completed the map of the coastline. The interior, however, was to remain practically unexplored for another 50 years.

Until the 1820s, most of the settlers in Australia were convicts. A few rich men had set up large farms and estates, and they employed convicts as labourers. In 1821, British government policy changed and ordinary settlers were allowed into Australia. The population grew rapidly as settlers poured in and, by the 1840s, most of south-eastern Australia had been divided up into farms and estates. The settlers had also established that, although they were part of the British Empire, they were going to govern themselves. A new nation was in the making.

Burke and Wills

Few of the newly settled Australians ventured far inland because the interior of the country was mainly a barren desert. There was so little information about the interior that, during the 1850s, the government offered a cash prize to the first person to cross Australia overland. Several people took up the challenge. The most famous attempt was that made in 1860 by a small expedition led by a police officer, Robert Burke, and a surveyor, John Wills.

Robert Burke led his expedition across Australia to disaster. He died on the return journey.

Burke and Wills set out in August with 12 companions, 23 horses and 24 camels to carry supplies across the Australian desert. After weeks of travel they left some members of the expedition and a store of supplies at a place called Cooper Creek, which they judged to be about halfway. Despite the fact that it was December, the hottest time of the year, they continued northwards, crossing deserts, plains and rocky hills, and becoming weaker all the time. Eight weeks later they reached the salt-water marshes along Australia's northern coast. Sick with thirst, they then turned south once more without actually seeing the sea, which they knew to be close. They were desperate to reach the supplies, 1100 kilometres away at Cooper Creek, before they ran out of strength. Under a blazing sun they struggled along on foot, but when they reached Cooper Creek they found from a sign cut into a tree that only eight hours earlier the other members of the expedition had given them up for dead and left. Both Burke and Wills died from thirst, hunger and exhaustion.

Parts of the Australian outback are so dry that it might rain only once every ten years.

One other member of the expedition also died. Another only survived because he was befriended by native Australians. He was found by a search party sent out to look for the explorers, and gradually managed to relate the sorry story of their fate. Two years later, in 1862, a team led by John Stuart successfully completed the first overland crossing of Australia.

Plant and animal surprises

Although Australia was a new land to Europeans, it seemed quite ordinary at first glance, especially around the southeast coast where the landscape looked rather like that of Britain. However, when Joseph Banks and the other naturalists looked more closely they soon discovered that the wildlife of Australia was definitely not 'ordinary'.

Some Australian plants were obviously related to plants found elsewhere in the world, which was just what the naturalists expected. But there were many other plants, such as the eucalyptus tree, that were new to science and which did not appear to be related to any known species. No wonder Banks became so excited at Botany Bay. If Australian plant life was surprising, then the animal life was astonishing. Neither Cook nor Banks nor any member of the crew knew what to make of kangaroos when they first saw them. In his diary, Cook asked himself how to describe an animal that looks like a deer, but jumps like a giant rabbit. Some of the other Australian animals seemed quite familiar — animals such as moles, wolves, bears and cats. But when specimens of these animals were examined closely they were found to be completely different from their European equivalents. The strangest discovery, made by

The egg-laying platypus is one of the world's strangest animals.

scientists who came to Australia in the 1790s, was the platypus, a furry, egg-laying animal with a beak. To the scientists of the day, the plants and animals of Australia were a real puzzle.

Separate evolution

The answer to the puzzle is that Australian plants and animals have a separate history from the rest of the world. Australia became an island many millions of years ago. At that time, there were two types of mammals — monotremes (that lay eggs), and marsupials

Kiwi land

New Zealand also has a strange assortment of native wildlife. Some insects have evolved to become much larger than usual. The giant weta, a member of the grasshopper family, grows to more than ten centimetres in length and hunts small insects in the undergrowth. Another strange creature is the tuatara, a unique type of reptile. Although it looks rather like a medium-sized lizard (about 20cm long), the tuatara is more closely related to extinct reptiles than to any living species.

Many birds in New Zealand took to living on the ground because there were no mammals to hunt them. Through evolution, the birds gradually lost the use of their wings. One of the most famous of these flightless birds is the kiwi. The kiwi is about the size of a hen, with a long thin beak which it uses to dig for earthworms. It has become a national emblem of New Zealand. A much larger flightless bird was the moa, which looked rather like a giant ostrich. However, moas became extinct shortly before Europeans arrived in New Zealand.

The flightless kiwi is still found in the forests of New Zealand.

The giant moa was hunted to extinction by Polynesian settlers.

(that give birth to embryos which develop in the mother's pouch). Later, a third type of mammal evolved — placental mammals that give birth to fully formed young. Placental mammals proved to be a more successful design than monotremes and marsupials, and in most parts of the world only placental mammals have survived to the present day.

In Australia, however, there were no placental mammals when the continent became an island, and it was the marsupials (and a few monotremes) that survived. The reason for this is that Australia was isolated, separated from the rest of the world by thousands of kilometres of ocean. This isolation also explains why so many Australian plants are different. All of the native Australian mammals are either marsupials or monotremes. The placental mammals that now live in Australia are all colonists that have arrived from overseas either by flying (bats), floating on logs (mice and rats), or in the company of human beings (dogs, sheep and rabbits).

A young kangaroo suckles milk from inside its mother's pouch.

Australian animals

The largest and most famous Australian marsupial is the red kangaroo, which stands about two metres tall. All kangaroos are herbivores (they eat plants) and the red kangaroo is generally found on open grassland.

The kangaroo is unique to Australia. Large jumping mammals are not found elsewhere in the world. Other Australian marsupials follow much more familiar designs. The marsupial mole looks and behaves exactly like moles in other parts of the world, despite being a completely different type of mammal. In the same way, marsupial cats, wolves and bears (koalas) look and behave very like other wild cats, wolves and bears.

In fact, this is not at all surprising. Although Australian marsupial mammals evolved separately from the rest of the world, they evolved in much the same way. A small mammal that specialises in burrowing underground in search of insects will evolve to look like a mole, whether it is a marsupial or a placental animal. In the same way, mammal predators (hunters) will evolve to look like cats and wolves. Australian marsupials are the best example of 'parallel evolution', in which the same animal design evolves separately in more than one place.

The marsupial cat behaves in the same way as true cats, hunting small animals for food.

The native peoples of the Pacific

A Polynesian double canoe of traditional design and construction. Sailing in boats like this the Polynesian people travelled from island to island.

Polynesian peoples

Cook was the first European to have extensive contact with all the various peoples of the Pacific. His observation that many of them were closely related has proved to be correct. Most of the Pacific peoples that Cook came across were Polynesians. Despite being separated by thousands of kilometres of ocean, the inhabitants of the Polynesian islands spoke related languages, used similar tools, and shared roughly the same beliefs.

The people who were to become the Polynesians set out from islands near New Guinea in about 1500BC. Sailing in canoes, and carrying all their belongings with them, they travelled from island to island. Little is known about these voyages into the unknown. But the skill of the Polynesian sailors is clear from the vast distances that they travelled in open canoes. Each time they moved on, they left

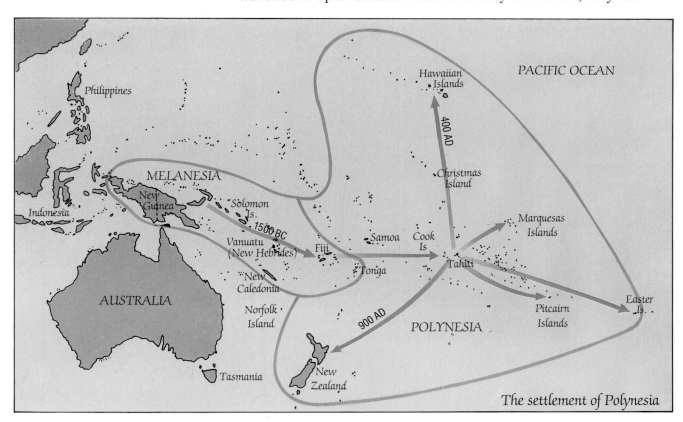

The settlement of Polynesia

some people behind as colonists. By about 1000BC, the Polynesians had reached the islands around Tonga. From here, the Polynesians continued their expansion. To the north, they settled the Hawaiian Islands in about 400AD. They reached Easter Island to the east at around the same time. The last area to be colonised was New Zealand, in about 900AD.

A thousand years ago, the Polynesians were the most widely settled people on earth. Although Polynesian territory consisted almost entirely of water, it covered an area of about 20 million square kilometres — twice the size of the present-day United States of America. The Polynesians were not, however, a united people. By the time Europeans arrived in the Pacific, in about 1500AD,

Traditional Polynesian houses are built from natural materials such as wood and grass.

each group of island settlements had developed separately from the others. There was some sea trade by canoe, often between islands hundreds of kilometres apart. However, the more distant islands were completely isolated. The inhabitants of Hawaii had long since forgotten that they once came from Tahiti, and the people of Tahiti knew nothing of the Polynesians in New Zealand.

Island life styles

As well as being skilled navigators, the Polynesians were also good farmers. The Polynesian settlers took dogs, chickens and pigs with them in their canoes, as well as seedlings of food crops such as yams, bananas and breadfruit. The sea was also an abundant source of food for the Polynesians. Many of the Pacific islands had shallow coastal lagoons which made excellent fishing grounds.

When Cook visited Tahiti, life was fairly easy for the native people. A family could survive with little effort by farming, fishing, and occasionally hunting for food. As a result, Tahitian society was fairly peaceful. Tahitian people were organised into tribal groups, each of which had its own territory and ruler. Relations between the different groups were usually quite friendly, but occasionally a dispute would lead to fighting and war.

In Tonga, which Cook admired greatly, life was less easy. The problem was that the population of Tonga had grown too large for the size of the island. The only way that everybody could be fed was by turning the whole island into farmland. This carefully organised agriculture was what so impressed Cook in Tonga. However, what Cook saw was the result of emergency measures necessary to feed the island's growing population.

The carved wooden figure of a Polynesian fishing god from the Cook Islands

Island paradises

Reports by Cook and other navigators who sailed the Pacific gave an over-simplified and idealised view of island life. Stories told by ordinary sailors, who often only went ashore for short periods of time, also tended to exaggerate the pleasant qualities of the island life styles. To those who listened, the islands of the Pacific, especially Tahiti, sounded like tropical paradises where everyone lived an easy life full of pleasure. But, in fact, the ordinary people of the islands often worked hard and went hungry.

The idea of a tropical island paradise in the Pacific became popular with the European public, and was taken up by writers and painters. Visits by islanders such as Mai (see page 26) added to this romantic view of tropical Pacific islands and their inhabitants. This enthusiasm continued during the 19th century. Some painters even went to the Pacific themselves, to paint island life as it really was. The most famous of these was the French artist Paul Gauguin who went to Tahiti in 1891. Gauguin painted beautiful but idealised pictures of Tahitian villagers.

Maoris

In contrast to the smaller islands of the Pacific, New Zealand was not a tropical paradise. The islands of New Zealand were larger, colder, wetter and more mountainous than the tropical Pacific

A painting of native Tahitians by the French artist, Paul Gauguin

A carved Maori *tiki* – a figure representing an ancestor-spirit that was supposed to bring good luck to the owner

Modern-day Maoris perform a traditional war dance with wooden clubs.

A portrait of a Maori chieftain showing the elaborate design of the tattoos on his face

islands. Many of the Polynesian food crops would not grow in New Zealand's climate, and the settlers had to rely far more on hunting for food. At first, the settlers' favourite prey was the moa, a giant bird which stood up to four metres tall (see page 30). The Polynesians became so good at hunting moas that within a few hundred years they had killed them all. By the time that Europeans arrived in New Zealand, moas were extinct.

The people of New Zealand are known as Maoris. Although they were of Polynesian descent, their society was very different from that of the other Pacific islands. Instead of living in peaceful villages along the coast, the Maoris lived in hilltop villages that were surrounded by protective walls of mud, thorn bushes and tree trunks. Maori society was much more violent than other Polynesian societies. Maori villagers were constantly raiding their neighbours to steal food, animals and human slaves. Because Maoris were used to fighting, they were not very friendly towards the first Europeans to arrive on their shores.

As well as being more violent, the Maoris also looked far more menacing than the other Polynesians. All Polynesians decorated their skin, usually just the skin on their arms. Maoris, however, tattooed designs all over their bodies, and especially on their faces.

Kooris

The native people of Australia are often known as Aborigines, which means 'the people who lived there originally'. Native Australians now prefer to be called Kooris. The Kooris are not Polynesians, and their history is much older than that of the Polynesians. The first human beings to reach Australia arrived about 35,000 years ago. These were the ancestors of the Kooris, and until the Europeans arrived their society developed without any contact with the rest of the world. The life style of the Kooris remained almost unchanged for tens of thousands of

A group of Kooris perform one of their traditional dances. The dancers have decorated their bodies with paint and bunches of leaves.

Koori art – a rock painting of a strange creature, probably an insect. Some Koori paintings depict the ancestor-spirits of Australian animals.

years. Most Kooris lived by hunting animals and gathering wild plants and insects for food. The Kooris knew how to make fire, but they had few tools apart from knives made from stone, wooden spears and boomerangs.

A boomerang is a flat L-shaped throwing-stick. Using a boomerang, a skilled Koori hunter can bring down a kangaroo standing 50 metres away. The special shape of the boomerang means that it can be thrown accurately along a curving path. The boomerang works because of the same scientific principle that makes an aeroplane wing lift an aeroplane into the air — a curved surface moving through the air creates lift. The Kooris made use of this principle thousands of years before the aeroplane was invented.

By the time Europeans arrived in Australia, Kooris had spread to all parts of the country. Most Kooris continued their nomadic life style, but this did not prevent them from having a strong sense of community. Sometimes, groups of Kooris would travel on foot for hundreds of kilometres in order to attend an important ceremonial gathering. The Kooris believed that the world was created by the dreams of their gods. These gods represented the spirit of each of the different animals in Australia. The Kooris believed that these ancestor-spirits were sleeping and dreaming beneath the ground. To the Kooris, the animals, the land and the gods were all one, and were all sacred.

Melanesians

The Melanesians are a third group of native South Pacific peoples. The Melanesians mainly occupied the islands nearest to New Guinea, while the Polynesians were found further east. In many ways, Melanesian society was very like that of the Polynesians.

The Melanesians grew the same food crops and raised the same farm animals (pigs and chickens). However, there were some important differences. Like most other human societies, the Melanesians had discovered the technology of making containers from baked clay. However, neither the Polynesians nor the Kooris made pottery. Instead, they used containers made from stone or plant material.

Easter Island

The people of remote Easter Island proved to be the most puzzling in the Pacific region. When the first Europeans arrived in 1722, the island had only a small population. The people of Easter Island seemed to have a very primitive life style. Yet the island was ringed with a series of huge statues, far bigger than any made on other Pacific islands. The biggest statues stood ten metres high and were made from a single piece of stone. How had these primitive inhabitants carved and moved such large stones? Some people have claimed that the Easter Island statues were made by people from South America or even from outer space, but scientists now have a more believable answer to the puzzle. The Easter Islanders are Polynesians who arrived by canoe. For many years their society flourished, but the population increased faster than the food supply and life became increasingly difficult. As the food shortage became worse, people banded together and built huge statues of one of their gods. They believed that the statues would persuade the god to supply more food. The food shortage became much worse and many of the population died. The survivors remained on the island, but their life style was much more primitive than before, and this was how the Europeans found them.

Some of the Easter Island statues are sinking slowly into the ground. Others have been restored to their original positions, complete with their 'hats' of different-coloured stone.

Horizons

You could find out about the following objects, ideas and places which all come from the native peoples of the Pacific: *mana* (magical power possessed by Polynesian gods); *tabu* (things or places that were forbidden to certain people); *lei* (Hawaiian flower garland); *hula* (Hawaiian dance); *tiki* (Maori carving of an ancestor); *corroboree* (Koori gathering); Ayer's Rock (Koori sacred place).

What happened later

A clash of empires

In 1789, ten years after James Cook was killed, the French people overthrew their king and set up an elected government. This event is known as the French Revolution, and is often used to mark a turning point in world history. The elected government of France was soon taken over by an army officer named Napoleon

A painting of the Battle of Waterloo, where the British and the Prussians finally defeated Napoleon. The British soldiers have formed a square to defend themselves against the French cavalry.

Bonaparte. Napoleon used the French army to conquer neighbouring countries such as Spain and Italy, creating a French empire in Europe with himself as emperor. However, Napoleon did not invade Britain, and Britain remained Napoleon's main enemy.

The Napoleonic Wars between Britain and France lasted nearly 20 years. During this time, the fighting spread to all parts of the world as both sides attacked the other's overseas colonies. At one point, Napoleon even devised a plan to invade Australia. In 1815, Napoleon was finally defeated by the armies of Britain and Prussia (a part of Germany) at the Battle of Waterloo in Belgium. At the peace conference that followed, Britain was rewarded by being allowed to keep all the French overseas territories that had been captured.

During the 19th century the British Empire became even larger. In the 1830s and 1840s new trading posts were established at Aden on the coast of Arabia, and on Hong Kong Island off the coast of China. Later in the century, Britain laid claim to large

Hong Kong in the 1890s

areas of southern and eastern Africa, and these territories also became part of the empire. However, the empire was not the only source of Britain's wealth and power. Britain was also the first country to introduce the widespread use of iron and steel and powered machinery into factories. This was called the Industrial Revolution.

The Industrial Revolution began during Cook's lifetime with the use of water power to drive textile machines, and the invention of the steam engine in 1769 by the Scottish engineer James Watt (1736-1819). During the 1790s a cheap method of making steel was invented. Other inventions quickly followed, such as the steam locomotive (1804) and the electric motor (1821). Within 50 years of Cook's death, Britain had modern factories turning out mass-produced goods.

Trade and navy

The combination of empire and industry meant that Britain soon came to dominate the world's international trade. But the success of the British Empire depended partly on the ability of British merchant ships to sail to any port in the world. In order to reach these distant ports on time, the merchant ships relied on charts made for the Royal Navy by expert navigators such as James Cook. Without accurate charts, international trade would have been a slow and inefficient process.

The last days of sail

The Industrial Revolution had an important effect on shipping. By the end of the 19th century, wooden sailing ships had mostly been replaced by metal steam ships.

During the first half of the century, wooden sailing ships reached the high point of their design. The fastest and most efficient ships were known as clippers, and they were used to carry expensive cargoes, such as tea and coffee, across the world. During the second part of the century, sailing ships with metal hulls became widespread. The coal-burning steam engine gradually replaced sails as a source of power. The last merchant ships to be powered by sails carried wool and wheat from Australia to Britain during the 1930s.

The *Ethiopian*, a clipper ship specially built to carry wool from Australia to Britain

The Royal Navy also played an active role in British trade. Although Britain remained at peace for most of the 19th century, the navy was on constant worldwide patrol to protect British ships against pirates, and to ensure that foreigners treated British ships and citizens with respect.

Breadfruit, the *Bounty* and Bligh

During the 1780s, the British government was forced to investigate the problem of feeding its workforce in various parts of the empire. The West Indies, which relied on slave labour during the 18th century, was a particular problem. Commercial crops, such as sugar cane, pineapples and coffee, all grew well in the West Indies. However, few food crops would grow in the tropical climate. The government decided to send a ship to Tahiti to collect seedlings of the breadfruit tree and take them to the West Indies. The ship chosen for this voyage was called the *Bounty,* and its captain was named William Bligh.

Bligh and the loyal members of his crew were cast adrift in an open boat. Some of the breadfruit plants can be seen on board the *Bounty*.

The breadfruit tree grows well in tropical climates and produces a fleshy white fruit. Although the fruit is rather tasteless, it provides a fairly nutritious food for humans. British officials thought that breadfruit would be an ideal food crop to grow in the West Indies in order to feed the slaves living and working there.

The *Bounty* sailed to Tahiti and collected several hundred breadfruit seedlings, each in an individual pot. However, Bligh was a bad-tempered captain who gave harsh punishments for the least offence. On the return journey trouble broke out when the crew mutinied (rebelled) against Bligh's authority. Captain Bligh, a few loyal members of his crew and some of the breadfruit pots, were put into a small boat and cast adrift in the middle of the Pacific Ocean. Somehow, Bligh managed to navigate this small boat over a journey of about 6000 kilometres to the island of Timor in Indonesia, which was under Dutch control. From there Bligh sailed back to Britain.

On board the *Bounty*, the mutineers returned to Tahiti where some of them stayed. The others took the ship to remote Pitcairn Island, where they were shipwrecked. They were the lucky ones. Those who stayed in Tahiti were soon captured by the British and hanged. Descendants of the survivors of the shipwreck still live on Pitcairn Island.

The mutiny did not affect the career of William Bligh. He made another trip to Tahiti to collect more breadfruit seedlings and deliver them to the West Indies. This voyage was a success, but the breadfruit experiment was not. In 1805, Bligh was appointed governor of the new colony of Australia. He was not a popular choice, and three years later there was a rebellion against his rule — another mutiny. Bligh returned to London where he died in 1817.

Australia

Rounding up sheep on a modern Australian sheep station

By 1850, there were about 400,000 settlers in Australia. During the second half of the 19th century the population increased

rapidly, largely as a result of immigration from Europe. By 1900, there were more than 3.5 million white Australians.

Although rainfall in most of Australia is low, there are large areas of natural grassland, especially in the eastern parts of the country. Settlers established ranches on these grasslands and raised huge numbers of cattle and sheep. Australian ranches are known as 'stations' and a single cattle station can cover more than 30,000 square kilometres. Large areas of grassland were also ploughed up for wheat. Around the coast, many fruit farms and orchards were planted. Not only was Australia able to feed itself, it could also provide Britain with a steady supply of wheat, wool and other agricultural produce.

Settlers panning for gold during the Australian gold rush of the 1850s

Australia also possesses great mineral wealth in the form of coal and metal ores. In the 1850s gold was discovered, starting

an Australian 'gold rush'. However, mineral deposits containing iron and nickel have turned out to be much more valuable. In the 20th century, Australia has also become a major producer of uranium, the fuel used in nuclear power stations.

The Kooris were not able to oppose the huge numbers of white settlers taking over their lands. Instead, they retreated from their lands until all that remained to them was the harsh Australian 'outback' (desert and semi-desert). During the 19th and 20th centuries, the Koori population has

Colonists out of control

When Europeans arrived in Australia, they brought with them plants and animals that had never existed in that country before. Most of these imported species were introduced into Australia without problems. But some other species were so successful that they quickly became pests.

A prickly pear cactus

The prickly pear is a quick-growing Mexican cactus. In Mexico, large numbers of insects and other animals feed on this cactus. The prickly pear was introduced to Australia because settlers thought that it could be used to make fences between their fields. The cactus did make good fences — for a short while. Then it spread to fill the fields, and kept on spreading. Within a few years, hundreds of square kilometres of land were covered with nothing but prickly pears. What the settlers had failed to realise was that there were no birds or insects in Australia that would eat the prickly pear, so it grew without check. This cactus is now considered a harmful pest in Australia.

decreased drastically. Many Kooris have died from European diseases; others as a result of hunger and mistreatment.

New Zealand

The British paid little attention to New Zealand until the middle of the 19th century. In 1840 there were fewer than 1000 white inhabitants on the islands, mostly traders, fishermen and a few Christian missionaries. But by the end of the 19th century the white population had risen to about 750,000 people.

As the Polynesians had discovered, few crops are suited to the landscape and climate of New Zealand. The Europeans, however, were able to bring with them domesticated sheep and cattle. The hilly grasslands of New Zealand were ideal for sheep and dairy farming. These types of farming quickly became the basis for the country's economy. In New Zealand today, sheep outnumber people 20 to one.

The native New Zealanders, the Maoris, resisted the invasion by European settlers. The Maoris were better organised and more aggressive than the Kooris, and they began to attack isolated farms, killing the settlers. In 1860, the British government sent soldiers to New Zealand, and for ten years the British fought the 'Maori Wars' against the native inhabitants. Peace was established in 1871, although the Maoris continued to be treated badly by the European settlers.

Modern times

Two world wars during the first half of the 20th century brought an end to the European colonial empires. Most overseas territories have now gained their independence, although the former colonial powers still control a few small territories in the Pacific Ocean, and the Hawaiian Islands are now part of the USA.

Australia and New Zealand remained part of the British Empire until it was abolished after World War II. Although they still maintain close relations with Britain, they have become increasingly independent as the patterns of world power and trade have changed. The countries that surround the Pacific Ocean have all broken away from Europe. Many of these countries are now world leaders in industry and trade. Australia, the state of California in the USA, Japan and Southeast Asia now have some of the most modern factories in the world. Modern-day Australians see themselves as part of a Pacific manufacturing and trading region that is almost entirely separate from Europe.

In recent years, the native peoples of Australia and New Zealand, the Kooris and the Maoris, have managed to make their voices heard. Their legal right to some of their traditional lands has now been recognised, and their ways of life are treated with far more respect. The recognition of 'native rights' in Australia and New Zealand started after the break up of the colonial empires. During the 1960s and 1970s, the peoples of Europe and North America once again became fascinated by native peoples. There was also a growing concern over the way that European industrial societies have polluted the environment and destroyed the ways of life of native societies.

In the 1760s, at the very beginning of contact with the Pacific island natives, Cook had worried that he might be corrupting them. Two hundred years later, people began to realise that Cook had been right to be so concerned.

Australian Kooris and their supporters stage a protest during the celebrations of the 200th anniversary of the founding of Australia, in 1988.

A statue of Captain Cook in Christchurch, New Zealand

Horizons

You could find out about the following people and places, which all have a place in the history of the Pacific region after Captain Cook: Ned Kelly (Australian outlaw); James Ross (first person to sail into the Ross Sea off the coast of Antarctica); Roald Amundsen (first person to reach the South Pole); Gallipoli (battle in World War I where many Australians were killed); Pearl Harbor (American base in Hawaii attacked by Japan during World War II); Bikini Atoll (site of nuclear bomb tests).

Glossary

boomerang A curved throwing-stick used by the native inhabitants of Australia.

botanist Someone who studies plants scientifically.

chart A sea map showing the shape of the coastline and the depth of water.

chronometer An accurate clock or watch.

convict Someone who has been convicted (found guilty) of a criminal offence.

Greenwich Meridian The line on a map (passing north-south through Greenwich, near London) which divides the world into east and west. Longitude is measured in degrees east or west of the Greenwich Meridian.

Kooris The native people of Australia, sometimes still referred to as Aborigines.

latitude Position on the earth's surface north or south of the equator.

longitude Position on the earth's surface east or west of the Greenwich Meridian.

mammal Any animal that has hair or fur, and feeds its young on milk produced by the mother.

Maoris The Polynesian people who settled New Zealand more than 1000 years ago.

marsupial A kind of mammal that keeps its young in a pouch.

Melanesians The native inhabitants of the islands near New Guinea.

monotreme A rare kind of mammal that lays eggs.

mutiny A refusal by soldiers, sailors or prisoners to obey orders.

navigation The art and science of knowing exactly where you are on a map, and how to find your way from one place to another.

New Holland The name given by Dutch sailors to stretches of the Australian coastline.

northwest passage A sea route that was supposed to exist between the Atlantic and Pacific oceans, around the top of Canada and Alaska.

outrigger A float attached to the side of a canoe or boat to make it more stable in the water.

parallel evolution The rule that animals that live similar life styles in similar environments will evolve to look like each other.

Polynesians The people who set out from near New Guinea and colonised most of the islands in the Pacific ocean, including Tahiti, New Zealand, Hawaii and Easter Island.

reef Underwater rocks built up from the skeletons of tiny coral animals.

scurvy A human disease that is the result of not having enough vitamin C in the diet.

ship of the line An 18th-century wooden warship that carried at least 60 cannon, and had a crew of more than 500 sailors.

Terra Australis The name given by the ancient Greeks to the continent that they imagined must lie south of the equator in the Pacific Ocean.

Index